The Garden Gate

ralph e. wierenga

 FriesenPress

Suite 300 - 990 Fort St
Victoria, BC, V8V 3K2
Canada

www.friesenpress.com

ISBN
978-1-5255-9064-1 (Hardcover)
978-1-5255-9063-4 (Paperback)
978-1-5255-9065-8 (eBook)

1. POETRY, SUBJECTS & THEMES, INSPIRATIONAL & RELIGIOUS

Distributed to the trade by The Ingram Book Company

Dedication and Invitation

With fond memories of a life shared
forever in my thoughts,
this book is dedicated to my mom, Aafke,
who gave me the inspiration in so many ways to use the countless gifts
that the living God has decided to bestow on my life.

With much joy and peace
within my soul,
with no regrets,
I first and foremost give honour to the living God, the King of kings
who made me
exactly who and what I am:
His child,
a royal prince in waiting.

Table of Contents

Foreword by the Author

Wrapped in the folds of these pages are the thoughts and experiences of Ralph Wierenga, so written to engage the mind in reflective thought for both friend and foe. Thoughts of a time when never a question was asked, yet inspired by the events of time, were so recorded to spark the thoughts of some of a precious time lost. Here recorded as an eyewitness of what has been seen and heard as a testimony of the greatness and power of my most treasured and honoured Friend that has walked with me through life. Common occurrences have been recorded over time through the thoughts and remembrances of a love so precious and dear that were rejected, and not acknowledged. Not a word of thanks was given. However, life's journey is recorded in two books that include every thought, word, and deed done with a selfless expression with room to fill in the gaps. Recorded dates could be important to some to gain the ideal impression and the depth of meaning. The God I serve knows it all. Every step and waking hour will be honoured with countless blessings, particularly when done for our parents. May you enjoy and be inspired to live life with a voice of gratitude and thanksgiving to the living God in such a way that all may see and be blessed accordingly.

WHY DID YOU COME?

What drew you to this spot right now?
What motivated you to open *The Garden Gate*?
Was it because of a friend?
Was it a suggestion of an acquaintance?
Or was it just another button to click out of boredom?
Do you know my name but don't really know me?
Did you ever ask what is this character all about?

How strong was your curiosity?

Can I take a peek through a crack within his life?
The gate is slightly ajar, dare I to look within?
What will I see?
What will I learn?
What can I draw from these scenes to understand?
How is this character living life?
Why so distant, so secret, so mysterious?

What was your motivation to be here at this moment in time?
What keys dangled in your hands to open this garden gate?
Did they work?
Will I never know if your eyes graced these words?
Will you dare to leave a note or allow your words to reach my ears?
Does the past bring you this close but no closer?
Is there something in your soul that wants to connect or reconnect?
Or does your pride hold you back?

Who truly can enter through this garden gate?

Who unlocks the gate to welcome you in?
Have you presented yourself to be welcomed in?
Are you able to give, or be vulnerable enough to share this time?
Are you willing to give up your comfort zone?
Are you willing to ask questions?
Are you willing to listen?
Can you recognize that my world is unique and different than yours?

Can you accept my world inside my garden gate?

Can you accept that inside the gate is my space?
Did you know that all that was and is built, created, dreamed, was a gift?
Can you accept that this was a gift maybe for you?
What have you done with that gift that was and is given so freely?
Can you accept without judgment what is displayed?
What are your thoughts now to the garden created inside this gate?
Are you able to say thank you for serving, surrendering, giving without limits?

For those farther in histories past, do you know what your actions have done?

Can you comprehend the depth of love surrendered?
Can you feel the tenderness of each seed tucked beneath the blanket of soil?
Can you feel the passion as the roots were laid in holes for new displays?
Can you imagine the joy of the impact on others—the surprise and delight?
Have you thought of all that was destroyed by a few words and actions, or not?
Did you help to build or destroy?
Did you help to encourage or break down?

Can you live your life without the influence of this garden?

The Garden Gate was written as an invitation
To share moments of the past, the present, and time to come
A love for nature, for life, for creativity
A passion for the living God
All inside and behind the gate
The toil to cultivate with drops of sweat and tears
Not for self
But all, just for you.

05/03/2020

Mother

MOTHER

In different worlds miles apart
A mother's love still binds the hearts;
On this day
A celebration of your motherhood
I, too, celebrate the gift
My Father gave to me,
You, my mom.

Recalling words of anger,
The wooden spoon at hand;
The hugs, the tears,
The times of silence, a look;
The exchanges of thoughts and ideas
All reflect the love you gave to me.

Though now worlds apart,
In spirit we are not.
My love to you, I trust is felt.
Believing,
The thoughts that link
Cannot express at will,
Are left for the Spirit to tell.

Your son
05/10/92

STEP BY STEP

One step, two steps
You're doing great.
"Do I turn right or keep going?"
Three steps, four steps
You're doing great.

I've got you from behind.
You're doing great.
You're going to make it.
That's it.

Excellent!
Do you need to rest in this chair for a bit?
Look at that!
You had not gone that far yet.
How exciting.

Ready to do a few more steps?
OK, let's do the round.
Are you ready?
Let's get you up.
One, two, three, hoops ahh.

One step, two steps, three
You're doing great, four.
I got you from behind.
You're doing great … nine, ten.
Take it easy.
We're in no rush.

Look at you! How many steps was that?
We made it all the way around the house.
We'll do a figure eight next time.
Wow, that was exhausting, heh?
We'll rest now.
Whooh! Wow!
Z
Z
Z..Z...Z....Z

12/2017

A LIFE CHERISHED

Up late,
Days, weeks, months, years
Giving comfort.
Just to be there visibly.
Companionship given daily.
What awaits beyond today?
Time will tell.
Is this another test,
The extreme degrees of sharing
Of His love and grace?
All for a soul that longs for fellowship
Yet hides it from others, but not from me.
Will years pass to see relief,
To see the Light shine?
Relief from all frustration and pain.
How much time must I give?
All is good.
Surrendering all of time and energy.
Unending with willingness.
What joy to give up all,
For the one I love, I cherish,
Till end of time—eternity.

04/27/2020

WAITING

Snuggled in her pink checkered blanket
Tucked all around
Warm and at ease
Patient
Waiting for the time
When the call to come home
Arrives without surprise

04/27/20

DETERMINED TO WIN

So cute
Melts the heart
With freshly curled hair
A smile to steal any soul
Big blue eyes
Firmly grips the rolling chair
Boldly walks about her home
Strong willed
Determined to win
As healing occurs
Faith is strong
Holding strong
Onto the God she loves

04/27/20

IN MY ARMS SHE LAY

For hours and days before
Looking into the distance
Seeing something glorious
That I could not see
I longed to see what I could not see
One day soon I too will see
Those clothed in glory
Waiting to take me home too

With her eyes on me
Her breathing slowed
Her entrance near
Do you hear the singing
Of those robed in white
Waiting for the right time
To bring you into our Father's arms
Where peace rest and joy unmeasured wait

The eyes a flutter gave
The time is near
The Holy Spirit's whisper
To sing that glorious chorus
"Hallelujah hallelujah
Hallelujah hallelujah"
Hesitation—staff near six or more
Begin I did a whisper ending load and clear

Words in song of praise for a time of ten or more
Till the breathing was enough
And her head in my arms lay
A silver crown about her head
A glorious peace ensued
Tears of joy tears of peace
As her body lay yet her spirit rose
To be free, free at last a long time in waiting

Looking back as being guided by the hands
Of angels rejoicing and sing
As another child is brought home
Seeing her son still bent over
Caressing her cheek
Closing her eyes with a gentle touch
Wiping her mouth so calm and sweet
A princess brought home at last

10/22/2019

6:38

At 6:38 the weekly alarm
As bells of a steeple ring

A reminder of a time
That will mark my life till the trumpet calls

A moment of remembrance
When a dearest love saw Glory

No, not merely saw Glory
But entered into eternal Glory

A time in life etched in my cells
That brings remembrance of a treasured past

Countless treasures of numbered years
Not of stuff, but treasures in the heart

Treasures etched on mind and soul
Of moments shared and words exchanged

Of plans and thoughts, ambitions, too
Of goals, ideas, and expectations yet to unfold

All these came to a sudden close
Yet God had other plans to carry them on

The approaching glory initiating three days before
As angels stood not far—waiting

Seen, but only by the one
Who would join them in a time not far

Following the gaze nothing was seen
Without a doubt only for the one to see

They were the focus
Until just before 6:38

09/12/18

ONE LAST TIME

One last time
I put to rest
The one I love.
Tucked in white silk,
Hands resting.
Her body in deep sleep
Waiting to be called
To rise one final time.
Meanwhile, night has fallen on her bed
I crank the lever down
She descends.
The tears blur the scene
But the memory is strong.
One last time
I've laid her to rest.
The closures were made
All is at peace.
No regrets.

06/22/2020

LOVE BEYOND MEASURE

In anticipation I wait
Knowing that the path of life
Is complete before me.
What will become of my remaining days?
Waiting, waiting, waiting.
Will I stay? Must I move?
The way has been prepared!
Trust is advised.
Not to retaliate.
All is known
By the One that matters.
A letter filled in accusations,
Assumptions, speculation
With no grounds for facts,
Or efforts to ask questions
For clarification, or for truth.
Doubting truth for personal gain
With words expressed to discredit.

Having no fear or anxiety
For the Lord God Almighty
Knows the truth,
Knows all that was given,
Knows the motives of the heart.

Those that oppose
Are filled with jealousy.
No control over such thoughts.
Each thinking wiser,
Each thinking all facts known.
Far from reality.
Fear not, says the Lord
Rewards will be given
In time.
Untruths, twisted facts
The Lord knows

Selfish greed.
In time, all things will burn.
All that is done in love
With selfless thought
Will be rewarded with crowns
To be laid at the feet of God
Before the throne.
Jeremiah confirms in 32
Of God's awareness,
And fights with strength
That eyes cannot see.
Faithfulness, selfless service
Love beyond measure.
Obedience will be honoured
No place or space for those
Who oppose and ignore.

There is freedom
There is peace
There is a calm
That stills the soul.
Relying on the One
Trusting in faith.
08/2019

REFLECTING ON A LOVE

Reflecting on a love
Eyes brimming with tears
A sorrow so deep
Who is there to love?

There is a call
To come down. To come down.
And fall on bended knees
Come down, come down, come down.

There is a call
To come down
To come down
To the crystal clear waters.

Come to the river
To drink of the water
That satisfies every thirst
And quenches the parched soul.

Come to the river
And satisfy your soul
With a love that only
God our Father can fill.

Come to the river
Replenish your depleted spirit
Refill and be lifted high
Stand pure, holy, in His sight.

Come to the river
That flows from the throne
Where God the Almighty resides
To satisfy your groans.

Come to the river
To give and to be given
A love so deep
Only a living God can give

Come to the river
To wash away your sorrow and sin
Drink deeply of the river
Where the love is so deep

01/15/2020

Spiritual

HEBREWS 10:35, 36

In a time when cut from the world I have known
In a city far from what I have called home

The book of Hebrews came to grace my eyes
And fill my mind with the power of our heavenly Father
Guiding in various ways.

Focusing on ourselves
To have confidence; to be confident,
To be sure,
Never doubting or wavering in our ability in Christ
To achieve this confidence,
We must believe,
Without a doubt,
In all the promises of God.
These are the keys
Of a focused life
Receiving untold blessings
From His giving hands
All to receive.

When I return home
I will explain what I have found
To be bottled up
In this very small part of the world.

1988 Chicago

CHOICES

When the world changes
Life takes its spins and twists.
What once was secure and firm
Shatters, and the security
Breaks and disintegrates.
It seems that all purpose and ambition
To carry on crumbles and falters,
Leaving a hole deep and wide
With little to hang on to
A future unknown.

No voice to share.
No ear to tickle.
No observing eye to watch
The raking of the blades.
The browning of the soil
Soft and fluffy,
Bursting with rainbows
Dreams of colour splashes
Deep scents and fragrances
Tickling the nose.

A man with earthly wisdom sought.
Shared my heart my loss.
Notes exchanged
Now with clout.
A name of standing and authority
Not a voice of weakness
Or "You're just the youngest."
Thank you, sir.
Now to wait for the outcome
From the voice of credibility.

Does the heart follow
Dreams of money
Or of stuff
That in time will shatter, fade,
Or wither?
Forgetting the values
Of love the surrendering of all
To give the best for one
For no replacement of a soul.

04/2019

A BROTHER NO MORE

Peace entwines each cell
Each living membrane
To the core
What joy soaks the inner soul
Though sadness fills
The minutes hours and days
That no man sees
A power and resolve
Is sure and pure
From a source without end

All said and done
Complete and total dependence
Given to the Almighty One
To guide and lead
Each step of the way
All alone no more
A companion for life
A support and strength unmatched
To demonstrate
The security in Him alone.

08/2019

DAY'S JOURNEY

As a sunrise gives way
To the anticipation of a new day
    and life itself.
So God's created beauty gives way
To the capability to identify the beauty,
    and the serenity of a sunset
Allowing the soul to rest with peace
To reflect on the day's journey
    with a thankful heart.

10/15/2019

ALL TO YOU

We are gathered as one
We are gathered as one
Lifting hands, outstretched arms to You
Praise the God that is alive
You are the one and only living God

Hallelujah
Hallelujah
Hallelujah

All together we stand
    Hallelujah
You deserve all the glory
    Hallelujah
Lifting You above all else
    Hallelujah
You are the only God we will worship
    Hallelujah

We stood alone yet all together one
We gathered with a few
Lifting our hearts our minds to You
Praising the God that is alive
You are the one and only God—You win

Hallelujah
Hallelujah
Hallelujah

Together we now worship
    Hallelujah
The King of kings Lord over all
    Hallelujah
Reigning supreme
    Hallelujah
We stand with You on solid ground
    Hallelujah

As one body Your bride
You the groom the King
We Your people, princes and princesses
Humbly bow with reverence
To You our Holy God

Hallelujah
Hallelujah
Hallelujah

Forever and ever and ever
 Hallelujah
To You all glory is lifted
 Hallelujah
God almighty, holy You are
 Hallelujah
All that we are we give all to You
 Hallelujah
Lord God Almighty all our worship is Yours

Hallelujah
Hallelujah
Hallelujah

05/21/2020

EMPTY HANDS

Empty hands I came
Empty hands I go

Going one day soon
Going to a place unknown

Unknown future
Trusting completely in faith

Faith that builds on faith
Living life now in complete expectation

Expectation, in awaiting God's perfect plan
A life filled with unexplained adventures

Adventures that brings others to the knowledge
Of the Greatest News ever heard or told

Told to ears that have never heard
Yet in a culture surrounded with the knowledge of the living God

God's timing is perfect in sharing the truth
To bring life to what was once filled with death

Death to life, life reawakening
Adventures laid open ready to serve

Service to the King of kings
To bring others into the fold of truth

Truth that spurs on more truth
As faith spurs on more faith

Faith that has no fear
Faith that is bold, pure, and true

True to the point of self-sacrifice
Solely to expand the Kingdom of God

God filling the empty hands
Heavy with the weight and the power of the Holy Spirit

06/30/19

SOMETHING REAL

How my heart yearns for something real
To worship
To acknowledge something greater than myself
I search for meaning
In places
In elements from nature
And try to connect and find a power greater then myself
I feel something but how to live to activate that source of power
I have searched and found but after a time I needed to find something else
It was not enough and I needed more to satisfy the emptiness in my inner self

With no relief I searched for truth and meaning
In the practices, rites, and rituals that many have found meaningful and true
I tried to follow and do as well as they but after a time the focus was on only what I
    did
A focus on routine and repetition with aimless repetitive words and so-called
    prayers
There was a striving to do what was right and to know what was wrong
But still after time my inner self still was not satisfied
By doing good and making every effort to avoid the wrong
Or the evil that was so prevalent in my inner self
I thought I was such a great and wonderful individual but for what?
I did good but for whom? Good for whom for what?
For what ultimate end did I strive to do well?
What was true? What was false?
Was my life meant to follow rituals and laws to please man?
I still felt so unclean and just so "yuck" despite all the good I did
There must be more but where and what will it be?
I feel so empty so purposeless
All my perfect words and deeds to no avail to fill the gap within
My heart feels so dark and unsettled
I needed more to satisfy the void

All the stuff, the money, the top-of-the-line name brands of this and that
I had it all, and yet, I still felt so empty and lost
I cannot be satisfied no matter what I do
I have done and gone both to and fro trying to fill the satisfaction of living
And yet I find myself so forlorn and depleted, if I do not gather more, as before

And then I came across a truth that only required me to believe
To believe the teaching with no do's or don'ts, but just to believe
To believe in a power greater than I, took a level of faith not necessary in my
    search till today
It seemed logical and true, realistic even, but do I dare to give up me?
This new concept required me to surrender all of who I was
All that I heard
All that I saw in the lives of those around me
Could it be true?
Ought I to allow this presumed living God fill my being with his
Holy Spirit?
What a thought!
How frightful to be filled with a Spirit not my own.
After so much time wasted in searching and giving reverence to this and to that
And still finding no hope or satisfaction in all the religious dead ends
What is there to lose?
So why not try this new concept? I have nothing more to lose yet so much more to
    gain
I took the step and accepted the sacrifice done for me—I was told
I only had to accept and believe this truth
The truth that all my sin, my crimes, the wicked thoughts and deeds have been
    washed clean
Not by what I have or not done, but what was done by this living God
Who sacrificed himself that I may live life now and into eternity
No ritual deeds or acts of goodwill, just to live life filled with gratitude and praise
    expressing thanks
My soul surrendered—my heart, my mind to this
To this assumed living God

I put all my strength into living life to serve, and in all things worship him
What more could I do out of gratitude for what he did for me

Oh, my!
Overcome with peace never felt before
Filled with spiritual comfort never before experienced in all my searches
A journey began of life's reflection of the need deep within,
For a cleansing from a holy Hand.

11/15/2019

YOU REIGN SUPREME
OVER ALL THE EARTH

1. Blessed is he who stands secure
    In the presence of the living God
    Who faints not but rejoices in His holy name
    Praise You Lord God Almighty
    You reign supreme over all the earth

Refrain:

    Hallelujah, hallelujah
    He reigns.
    Hallelujah, hallelujah
    He reigns.
    Hallelujah, hallelujah
    He reigns.

2. Sending light to us far below
    Securing our faith forever more
    As we toil and labour to honour Him alone
    Praise You Lord God Almighty
    You reign supreme over all the earth

Refrain:

    Hallelujah, hallelujah
    He reigns.
    Hallelujah, hallelujah
    He reigns.
    Hallelujah, hallelujah
    He reigns.

3. Forever we bow to Your name
    Raising our arms our hands to Your throne
    Filling us with renewed hope to face each new day
    Praise You Lord God Almighty
    You reign supreme over all the earth

Refrain:

> Hallelujah, hallelujah
> He reigns.
> Hallelujah, hallelujah
> He reigns.
> Hallelujah, hallelujah
> He reigns.

4.   For evermore His guidance waits
        Seeking out His favour to the end
        That my soul finds peace entering His glory pure
        Praise You Lord God Almighty
        You reign supreme over all the earth

Refrain:

> Hallelujah, hallelujah
> He reigns.
> Hallelujah, hallelujah
> He reigns.
> Hallelujah, hallelujah
> He reigns.

5.   Seemingly the darkness rules all
        All dread of isolation no more
        Waiting for the day You once again show Your face
        Praise You Lord God Almighty
        You reign supreme over all the earth

Refrain:

> Hallelujah, hallelujah
> He reigns.
> Hallelujah, hallelujah
> He reigns.
> Hallelujah, hallelujah
> He reigns.

6.   You alone, blessed Saviour trust
     Only You can see us through divine
     Entering into Your heavenly light glorious
     Praise You Lord God Almighty
     You reign supreme over all the earth

Refrain:
     Hallelujah, hallelujah
     He reigns.
     Hallelujah, hallelujah
     He reigns.
     Hallelujah, hallelujah
     He reigns.

04/16/2020

BEYOND

Tiptoeing through the crystal drops
Raining down in glittering splendour
Tails that disappear into the heavens
Euphoria to the highest degree
A carpet of diamonds stretching beyond
A bucket in hand to collect—nothing
Drinking in the scene a memory to hold
These dropping spheres lighting the way

02/15/20

FREE INDEED

Tempted but sinless
A scapegoat
To set me free
Guilt and shame
No hold on me
Free, yes, truly free

04/29/2020

THERE IS SUNSHINE
IN MY HEART TODAY

There is sunshine in my heart today
As God gives voice to his truths
Rolling words off my lips
To touch the hearts of each that come
To see the light to hear the truth
Of him who came
To wash our sins away
To comprehend this fact
Before the definitions are procured
Comprehension of this Book
This God
How stressful this can be
A voice to speak
To clarify
To bring down the walls of anxiety
Unplanned not memorized
As truths are unwrapped
Understanding seeps in
Clarification makes clear
The uncertainties of this strange Book
That swings wide the doors
So that God will open their minds
To understand the scriptures
Flooding the darkened souls
With a brilliant light
That brings peace and calm
What once was dark and troublesome
Of fear and uncertainties
To a joy that passes all understanding
Filling pockets of void
Saturating the heart with everlasting sunshine.

Now I am spiritually drained.

A refilling is required.

11/19/2019

MAJESTY!

Majesty, majesty, majesty
Oh, the majesty of the One and Only,

The mountains crisp and clear
White capped against a spring blue sky
Majesty in all its bold beauty.

The air, sharp, clean
Mountains all around
Secure.

The fields in swaths of white and strips of green
Waiting in peace for spring to take root
In rays of warming sun.

The calm and peace that rest the soul
Preparing the day in giving aide
Filling souls with understanding.

Oh, the majesty of it all
The peace that fills my soul
When life's stresses are replaced.

The hands held high in spirit
While the soul sings
Glory hallelujah.

03/20

IN A
BOX

We like to put things in boxes
To store
To hold
To contain
To conceal
To forget
To treasure
To display
To set limits
To retain memories
To ...

Boxes are often cardboard
But tin, plastic, or wood can do
Better strong than weak
Before it's on the floor

Some things don't need boxes
To be stored
Their sizes too large to be contained
Or just an awkward shape

There are parts of our lives
That should never be contained
The first is love
The last relationships

When these are boxed
They confine and restrict
They cause limitations
Fear, frustrations, and fatigue

There is one element in life
That can never be boxed
Though man sets limits
To restrict, and hold back its freedom

Freedom to share—now
Freedom to be heard
Freedom to touch lives
Freedom to change souls

Many try to box the Holy Spirit
Resulting in limitations and ineffectiveness
Because my time, my way, not now—
Are often first considerations

No box can hold or contain
The Holy Spirit's power
Or how it moves
Always outside the box with great surprise

Boxing efforts of the Holy Spirit
Sets limitations
For miracles
For growth
For friendships
For change
For encouragement
For lives renewed
For souls to be filled
For brokenness to be restored
For hope to be fulfilled

04/2019

THE SOUND OF ANGELS SINGING

The day was long
The day was quiet

It was a day for perfect reflection

To meditate

On what I had learned
    and received

    Meditate

On what I had heard
    and seen

    Meditate

And when I do these things
Day by day and not just for today

To each the same
In God's Holy Name

Then, then…
I don't believe it!

(Did you hear? Oh, listen!

Can you not hear it?

Oh, the harmony! The clarity! The voices of praise!
No breathing breaks through every hallelujah)

Peace is with me.

Oh, yes!

Peace now fills my heart
My soul

The comfort of the presence of the Holy One in my space
Is his space.

04/2019

WORTHY, WORTHY, WORTHY IS THE LAMB

Worthy, worthy, worthy is the King
Who rules the heavens and the earth.

Worthy, worthy, worthy is the Lord of lords
Who reigns in majesty and glory untold.

Worthy, worthy, worthy is Emmanuel
Who dwelt with us a time without sin.

Worthy, worthy, worthy is He
Who became man that I may live.

Worthy, worthy, worthy is the Lamb
Who shed his blood that my soul may not die.

Worthy, worthy, worthy is the One
Who descended into hell for me.

Worthy, worthy, worthy is God Almighty
Who cleansed me of my sin.

Worthy, worthy, worthy is the Son of God
Who made a way to give eternal life.

Worthy, worthy, worthy is the Holy One
Who raises man to worship and adore Him.

Worthy, worthy, worthy is the living God
Who pleasures in the saturation of praise.

Worthy, worthy, worthy to Him
Who is an ever-present God.

Worthy, worthy, worthy is the Creator
Who deserves all honour, praise, and glory.

Worthy, worthy, worthy
May my soul rest in His presence daily.

Worthy, worthy, worthy always
Singing praises to and in His name.

Worthy, worthy, worthy forever
May I be found worthy is His sight.

Worthy, worthy, worthy
To be called a child of the living King

Worthy, worthy, worthy eternal
Hallelujahs to the risen Christ

Worthy, worthy, worthy Holy Spirit
Who came to fill longing, empty souls.

Worthy, worthy, worthy is Jehovah Jireh
Who provides my every need.

Worthy, worthy, worthy is Elohim
Who is the true and only God.

Worthy, worthy, worthy He who is called Rapha
Who binds and heals my wounds.

Worthy, worthy, worthy is He the Ra'ah
Who is the only way to truth, my shepherd.

Worthy, worthy, worthy is Yeshua
Who rescues and delivers me to freedom.

Worthy, worthy, worthy
With hands raised high.

Worthy, worthy, worthy always
Giving glory, honour, and praise.

Worthy, worthy, worthy
How my soul rests in this thought.

Worthy, worthy, worthy knowing
The comfort that I am His and His alone

Eternal praise is due His name
Hallelujah! Forever hallelujahs!

11/2019

WORDS OF TRUTH

Send the light in this time of darkness.
What glorious reminders in the Word
Of the hand that controls the comings and the goings,
The ups and downs, the twists and turns
That confuse the rhythm of life
All has a divine purpose that in time will comprehend
Stages of growth painstakingly must endure
Life's uncertainties and challenges
What a glorious understanding is given
That no need to fret is genuine
When submission to the Holy One is surrendered
And the fretting of the plan and uncertainties are straightened
To a calm journey from the tossing and turning
Assisted by the calm spirit of trust.
The rollercoaster stabilizes and the butterflies are settled
As the reliance and hope is strengthened.
The changing winds of life's living become emboldened
Followed by a refocusing on the distant goal.
What an ecstasy to depend on a God
Who lives and has all things in his hands.
With a bowed head and a surrendered heart
Submission to his ways is the rock
That never trembles or shakes.
Boldly, standing erect in posture, a voice without shame
Proclaiming words of truth
Seldom heard in wind or breeze.
Without fail the victory is won
As promised by the resurrected One.

01/2020

"I AM HERE"

In this time of quiet
Let my daily diet
Be fed from Your word
That You may be heard
Not through the storm
But through great form
Not through a roaring fire
But gently through a lyre
Let me hear Your gentle whisper
So powerful as a river
Through all the tears
When I face doubts and fears
All I want to hear
Is "I am here"

04/20/2020

OH SACRED HEAD NOW BRUISED

Oh sacred head now bruised
For days he was accused

Shunned by all but a few
He took it all for us to be new

What language ought I to use or none at all
To give thanks for wiping clean sins, since the Fall

To give thanks for the sacrifice of Your only Son
As he alone could be the one

To set us free from guilt and shame
Without blame

Death has occurred
On Golgotha's stone ensured

The payment for sin
That we may win

When blood and bile poured from his side
Down through the crack did find

The Ark of the Covenant
To cover the Mercy Seat extravagant

As foretold of old
We will not be controlled

When dawn breaks through eastern skies
New life came forth—renewing ties

For death now has no sting
As we are lifted with his wings

To heights beyond
As we respond

With peace and calm
From Gilead's balm

04/12/2020

SEVEN WEEKS OF OMAR

Seven weeks of Omar
Anticipation waits in the last of the seven sevens
Soon the weeks will end
Then the Golden Year has come
The Golden Year of Jubilee

In symbolic expectancy
The barley stems accumulate
From one to forty-nine
When the final barley stem is collected
On display to make it fifty

First there is doubt
Then complete and utter unbelief
As reality sets in
That humanity has been blindsided
By the removal and a twisting of the holy days and weeks

Awakened humanity will be
To the Year of the Golden Jubilee
Set free, yes, set completely free
The one-hundred-twentieth Jubilee has come
The promise of our living God fulfilled

Standing now in awe
That this generation is to see this day
When Satan and his chosen come down
To fall before man and the face of God
In shame and utter wretchedness into the abyss

When humanity stands firm
In the Word of the living God
Setting free from terrene enslavement
Blinded by trickery and lies
Laid bare to set humanity free

Rejoicing now together praise
The living God over all he reigns
Freedom brings
To all who bow in reverence bring
To the One who sitteth on the throne

05/25/2020

CONTEMPLATION

Lost
I sit gazing
Trembling for no cause
Uncertainty of the days to come
Not anxious or worried
Just plain lost
Empty
Contacts distant few and far between
A screen for some to communicate
Disinterested lost
Uncertain of what is to come
Lost

Though lost
There is an inner peace that fills
The hollow cavities
There is a reassurance in the Word of God
That reminds to remain
Steadfast, pure, and true
Steady goes the course of life
Day after day,
Week after week
And on …
Yet, a peace resides within the soul
Of the promises of God
That he is always near
All but a whisper
And he is there
Trusting in obedience
One day at a time
Knowing that a plan he has
All perfectly laid smooth
For my feet to tread
Though lost I feel
Assured I am

That God is in control.
No fear or doubt may enter in
For then the gate is wide
For Satan and his tricks
To deceive and manipulate
Causing crevices and pits to appear
Falling
Stirring unrest, creating fear
But when the light of heaven shines
Strong,
No shadows lurk about,
But hope and expectancy,
A smile broad and true
Graces the face in his image made
Firm and sure
Love abounds
As each day evolves.

What is lost
When Christ the Saviour
Dwells within?
A fleeting moment of uncertainty
But then it is gone.
Lost no more but always found
Within his arms,
His hands, he guides
Strength empowered
Daily gives to every cell.
To be a child
An adopted one
Made whole and pure
Brought to his side the King.
What am I, a prince he made
And for you a princess
All with uncorrupted royal blood

Lost no more
His I am.
A purpose given strong and free
For I am his
And he is mine.
What joy now fills those moments,
When sliding down a slope
Of self pity
Yet all along not lost at all
For God the King
He reigns within.

05/26/2020

ARE WE THERE YET?

Have you seen the tree outside your door,
Stretching its limbs across the floor
Out into space to breathe?
Can you hear the cells scream,
As they multiply at speeds extreme
Creating limbs, increasing, unfurling into new leaves?
With anticipation carbon dioxide clings
Purifying air for lungs to have wings
To keep life pure and free.
A light so bright
To keep the fight
The air so clean.
Everything overshadowed with dappled green
A hue so rich and pure
That any sickness can have a cure
Resting in the calm
In the centre of His palm
Glory hallelujah—love the peace
A time to celebrate with a feast
Beside the river of life
And trees with fruit that ends all strife
Month by month new fruit they bring
Accompanied by voices of multitudes sing
Bringing calm, peace, and glory
As every note tells His story

05/30/2020

Life

DELUSION/ILLUSION

are you walking in delusion
living life in unknown falsehoods
following the masses
as if it were the truth

consume, consume, consume

it is good, they say it is,
everyone is doing/saying/singing
so it is okay

do you follow or do you lead?
do you trust and believe
in you, the individual?

are you one who questions
or one who goes along with the masses
without a thought
of another way that may be
better, purer, safer,
holier?

many walk in delusion
with no thought to think deeply
independently
but walk blindly saying
yes, yes, yes

one must have tolerance
is the rhetoric
deceiving others and themselves
becoming a follower all in time

blinded by "tolerance,"
independent thinking
falls to the wayside
as fear of being different
isolating from the masses

the book of truth
is a better choice to follow
to remain outside the masses
to avoid the life of disillusion,
are you free?

02/09/20

IN THE MIDDLE OF THE STORM

In a storm
Wild
Tossing to and fro
Unstable
Hanging on
White knuckles
Desperate.

Set me free
Pleading
Yet, beyond the bow
It rages fiercer
All noises of desperation
Seeking to destroy.

Inside the bow
Safe
Though tossing
Winds a-raging
How to stand?
Cannot
But on knees
Can stand
In the middle
Of the storm.

Lifted up
Able to stand
Bold
Strong
In the storm.

The Master
Of the storm
Hears the cries
Fills the fears

Of the storm
With calm
Bringing peace
Standing firm
With unseen
Hand
Resting
Upon the shoulder
Emitting strength
That flows
Deep
Strong
Renewed courage
To face
The storm.

Uplifted
The storm
No longer
Billowing
But just a wind
Gentle
Not to sink
But to toss
Reminding
Keep on trusting
Renewing the faith
Hearing the voice
Beyond the storm.

Waiting
Weary
Trusting
Embracing
Still waiting
To gently
Land upon the shores

Refreshed
Enlightened
Emboldened
To face
A new day
Sharing the greatness
Of the wisdom
Of the Master
Of the storm

02/15/20

SPRING FRAGRANCE

There is a fragrance in the air
The intake of breath not so fair
The odours of spring freshness
But rather of our rural uniqueness
Ahh, the waves of freshly cut hayfields
Swaths of green grass yields
Fresh, clean, a breath for all day
That fills this month of May
Then came the rake to scatter
The blades of grass that causes catarrh
Twirling wheels with prongs
Creating a clickety-clack whirring of afternoon songs
Scattered, the sunrays dehydrated
Nutrients preserved and mitigated
In swaths again they lay
To gather for silage not for hay
And just as quick as the heat of the day
Tractors with barrels the size of a house
With a liquid the fields to douse
To fertilize for the summer crop
It could not help but make you stop
With every breath through nose or mouth
Filling all senses with such couth
In an arc it did spray and fall
That sent out many a call
Of man beast and fowl
Of the air that was so foul
The news has spread
Of the air that lingers with dread
There is no escape
That results with much agape
Until the rains in May come down
To take away the frown
Of a city and a valley
That held this spring fragrance, as if in an alley

05/08/2020

AS THE HOURGLASS TURNS

A life of creativity
Filling lives with colour and beauty
Shadows and light
Taste buds to tickle
Alcoves of solitude
A friend or two or more
A cup of tea or coffee
A biscuit, sweets, or more
A delectable delicate sandwich
Now but a memory
A dream shattered
Heartless and cold

As the hourglass turns
A renewed focus ensues
For whatever time remains
New memories need creating
Somehow done inspirationally
To touch lives for Christ the King
That will last eternally

Never a dull moment
When ambitions are set
What a goal to be reached
What a responsibility to take hold
What a reward awaits
When the tasks are complete
A glittering crown
Laid at his feet

04/14/20

SEEDING

A handful of seeds
Some look similar
Others so different
Yet in the heart of every seed
A spiritually implanted knowledge
Of what that very seed would produce

A handful of seeds
A task for the distributor
One by one reverent
Planted for each to succeed
A higher input not from college
For our bodies to use

A handful of seeds
Each row particular
A label so prevalent
A hoe and rake proceed
To eliminate the smallage
Along with the invaders

A handful of seeds
The peas form a reticular
But always behaving benevolent
Always yielding to exceed
Beyond the ability to acknowledge
With a pull the pod let loose

A handful of seeds
Some are orbicular
To share what is relevant
Or for mammals to feed
That used to pull a sledge
Waiting for the garden to produce.

04/15/2020

WWG1WGA

Together we are one
Standing tall
Though not fun
Waiting for justice to fall

The movement surges
It cannot stop
As crimes emerge
Through Q drops

On a daily basis
Calling out to Red Pill
Ever-new faces
Using chess skill

Discerning with Q
His help to confirm
Held together as glue
Causing others to squirm

When evil emerges
Crimes to unfold
QAnon's worldwide urges
To end this stronghold

Never to be dismayed
Though many be confused
They will all be paid
For what was misused

Darkness to light
Slavery to freedom
Growing with more might
Punishment for treason

Patience a must
As we wait with honing
As they go below the crust
Revealing with great groaning

When young lives emerged
Never seeing the light of day
Because they were submerged
Before there was a way

A man was ordained
To take down worldwide
All evil it contained
With fewer than ten he did confide

Through all the prayers
Of saints nationwide
All the tears that are shared
Brought victory in a huge tide

As a final fourth attack
A hufan virus did swarm
It seemed to be so black
To create an uncontrolled storm

But every people cool and calm
Waited out the time
Waiting on the psalm
That frees us from the filthy grime

In the middle of its centre
Was the celebration
Of the King of kings
His death and resurrection

Bringing new joy and hope
Rising far above
No longer viewing life with limited myope
But soar far and wide as a mourning dove

Seeing anew the scope of life
Sharing love beauty and peace
Releasing all the created strife
Giving all those living a new release

WWG1WGA
HELLELUJAH TO THE LIVING KING

04/12/2020

TO JOURNEY DOWN LIFE'S PATH

There are paths in life
Where one gazes, reflects, contemplates
And ultimately decides on one
With great excitement or drudgery to follow

The decision on which path to embark
Depends on factors
Are you a follower, a leader, or an adventurer?
Or do you travel your path just because?

Was the path you're heading down
Wiggling through, scraping by
Given, handed down, or assigned to you
Without dramatic flare and pomp?

Are you thinking of other possibilities
Of paths other then the one that you are on
Filled with regret, curiosity or wonder
If there is another way?

Is the path you are on because of someone else's greed
Lack of compassion, love, consideration
Or some other "I" centredness
That left you out and dangling?

Such is I.
All dreams, passions, and expandable ideas
Taken, robbed, sent packing
To where? To what? For how long?

What to do now? Stuck for a time
Reflecting, evaluating, pondering
The options that can be taken, had
With the potential time that remains in life

Do I hunker and huddle
Or go on a limb
Begin afresh
Rebuild from scratch?

My spirit is calm,
My will is adventurous
A follower I am not
A quiet leader I am

Excitement I need
With the possibility to dream
Expand and build
To see new life emerge, coming forth

In all, for others to enjoy
To share, to experience an awe
To motivate and inspire
To hear the words "So cool!"

As Frost once hinted at:
Will I take the path less travelled?
Yet others have taken equally
Never to look back but step forward

Embracing each day anew
Challenges embracing
Becoming stronger and more wilful
Building afresh, dreams, hopes, ambitions—life itself

Building not on self
But building on a Rock
That aligns each step, each choice, each of life's seconds
To correspond to the ultimate plan that builds for eternity

05/12/2020

LIVING LIFE ANEW

Room by room a slow process of emptying
Filling boxes of life's treasures again and again.
Boxes piling high, row upon row
Filling up other space that was empty
Carpets rolled tight all ready to be loaded

Life changed once filled with living life
Serving, loving, surrendering, giving
All done with no thought for personal gain
Left with rejection, accusation, unverified false truths,
Words that deemed to lift high self and put down the other

Trust and respect lost, empty of bonds that blood binds
Waiting and seeking those to retie
Cords of friendship based on truth and respect
Does such exist? Or is this grabbing on strings that snap
One such relationship exists holding trust, respect, and truth—God.

Old rooms emptied, new rooms filled
Boxes once filled are now being emptied
Resuming life with vigour and purpose
Arranging and aligning to resume living life
To serve, love, surrendering to love once again.

What a joy to live again with cords cut loose
The freedom to be free
The space to move unrestricted to do to be
What the inner soul expresses to be real
Arms outstretched to receive, to give, to be renewed—living life anew.

What joys awaits?

07/2019

FREE

Free and to hold freedom is enriching
When a sign calls out in boldness *FREE*
We are drawn as to a magnet
Becoming as slivers of metal
Being dragged pulled or lifted
Temporarily by the magnet
Into a bondage
To
Something
Before
Something was/is free
It was bought under and for a price
Then used possibly abused
In time it is torn snagged
Cracked chipped
Shattered
Useless
Helpless
Until
In hands
Molded with love
Mends "gestopt"* hides
Glued reshaped renewed
Though scarred for life and time
Initially hidden pretending for a time
As if it is new and fresh from being manipulated

From free to freedom without ropes or shackles
From bondage to freedom that sets the soul to fly
A joy and contentment seeps in to mend what was torn
The cracks and covered chips the scars of life are mended
Truly mended through grace that abounds
Forgiveness extended grace ever flowing
A peace that enfolds ever greater to fill and flood the soul
To reach out to the hurting the broken the fallen

Restoring to heal to be bold strong courageous to have victory
Through the working of the peace and love that goes beyond our
human understanding
Oh, the joy
It is truly free to bring freedom

09/13/19

*gestopt (Dutch): The finished task of mending a worn out sock,
e.g. the heel or the sole of the sock.

A WEDDING FEAST

The friendship
The love
The joy
The saturation of your presence
Filing my soul to overflowing

To walk
Hand in hand
To embrace
You are my very being
Each day over and over again

To celebrate
Your commitment to me
And me to you
Setting plans
To live life as one

Then the day
Of truth unfolds as
A public commitment
Is told
With witnesses to hold true

The table set
The food prepared
The water poured
Or is it divine wine
The tastes are all sublime

The greetings
The congratulations all around
The chatter, the laughter
And tears, too
As fellowship soars and wanes

Farewells are shared
The journey begins
Adventures to unfold
Unique
To the two to behold

05/18/20

AGGRAVATION

AgGravation one or six
Man look at that
He's out already
Not another three
And yet again a four.

Around the board we go
And to base you go!
With a six and in the middle you go
And now to wait for one
Or out you're kicked by one.

Look at that
He's got two in base so quick
And I have three still at home
A four a five or even a two
But never a one or six.

We laugh and go on
As each get a turn
Rolling a die
Making nicks in the table
Week after week.

V is so red with frustration
When winning she does not get
J often wins in quietness rolling white
While E in orange is even quieter
But wins almost equally the same.

J in bright shining yellow
Attempts to bring to base
But often stuck at home
While R is decked in green
Most often last but laughs the same.

How fun to spend a night
In fellowship with saints
As family gathers round the table
Sharing life and a poem or two as well
Ending with words of praise to the Father of all fathers

11/3/2019

THE GRAVITY OF HOME

Walking down the sidewalk
Beside a white picket fence
Interweaved with climbing roses
Of pink, white, red, and yellow.
The air was fresh
The shadows long
With the promise of a warm
Cloudless blue sky.
The lawn was green
The maple trees tall
Arms spreading wide
Walking through the dappled shade.
The gravity of home
The calm, the peace, the warmth
Entwined in all the senses
Ahh!
Always a smile when approaching the front door.

04/2020

SPACE

Space:
So much space
Yet no space at all.
What is mine?
What is theirs?
Not to touch or move
Pointing fingers to avoid

My comfort corner
Is my space
That is mine.
I curl up in my chair
The Bible in one hand
I am safe—trusting

2018

THUNDERCLAP AWAKE

Winds blew fierce
Smashing drops of rain
Against the window pane.
Clattering nonstop
A soothing steady clicking
That arises doubts
Whether the melted sand
Will hold the water and wind.
Gusts of wind
Pelting drops of rain
A shifting curtain
The house not airtight.
As I sit book in hand
The lamp a gentle mellow yellow glow
Flickers once then twice
But steady goes.
A clap of thunder
A rattle of windows.
Something fell from the mantle.
A jerk, a jump
The book lay open on the floor
Pages fanned
All is well
Nothing broke.
Another clap and rolling thunder
Darkness suddenly invading space.
The flickering flames of the fireplace
Guided to the drawer of candles
Matches in hand
A spark. A flash. A flicker. A steady glow
Dancing shadows kept me company
As oil lamps were lit.
A steady glow and all is bright
Time to quietly sit, relax

Watching the flames dance
Sipping the mug of lukewarm coffee.
An empty glass of red wine
Almost invisible.
Time passed reflecting on life
People, plans
Dropping eyes
Distant thunder
Rain no longer attacking windows.
A steady gentle rain ensued.
Time for bed.
Lanterns out.
One in hand.
Fireplace low a steady flame a-flickering
Up the stairs railing in hand
Lantern in the other
Sheets pulled back
Crawling in
Tucked warm and snug
Safe from the tempest
Rain, wind, and lightening
The soothing steady drumming of the rain on roof tiles
A nursery rhyme of sorts
To sleep soundly fell.

06/23/2020

SUMMER FUN

In the green shadows of the trees
A sky-blue children's pool
Nestled in the blades of summer green grass.
A fluorescent green garden hose snaked from the faucet.
Erupting splashes.
Children's screams and laughter,
Creating fun of nothing
With no concern in life
But to soak in the cool waters
In the summer dappled light.

06/24/2020

A TWIST IN NARRATIVE

When darkness falls evil dies
When light shines darkness dissipates

Last breaths of darkness
Fling the last throes of life
With force fear to evoke
The final breaths of life
In gasps
Hanging on
To what remains
Seemingly of great power
Suddenly
Without warning
Collapsing
Spent
Nothing
Darkness thought it had strength
Was the weakest link of all.

The light—strong
Power, strength, and endurance
Master of them all
A pinprick pierces the darkness
Growing in fierce force
Gaining
Light overtaking
Radiating
Overpowering
Winning
Victory in hand
Victorious

Illuminated
No longer blind
Awakened by the light
Ability to see with clarity
The full spectrum
That was once hidden by the darkness
Light brings life
Eternal ever burning light
Radiating 360
The gift of sight with light
To guide and lead
Safety
No fear.
Freedom to the core
Through the strength of the light.

06/30/2020

Nature

GARDEN GATE

As I was wandering through the gardens,
I came upon a gate painted a deep, warm blue.
There was a path that led me clearly to this gate;,
However, the gate had no handles.
The gate was shut tight
With no means to open to reach the other side.
On either side of this blue painted gate
There was a fence with no gaps to squeeze through.
Between the fence boards and posts on either side
And the space above the gate
Were vines twisting and clinging
As if they were holding everything all together.
I pushed and wiggled the gate panels,
But the gate did not give way.
It moved but was solid in its place.
There was a crack in the centre of the gate
Just wide enough to peer through.
What I saw drew my desire ever more to reach the other side.
But how?

Beyond the gate the path continued
Under an arbour covered with vines
Of China doll and creeping jasmine.
The fragrance of the jasmine flower
Wafted through the fence boards
To the garden on the outside.
Along the path were large bushes of hostas
And other creeping things.
The calm and the dappled green shade
Brought me into another world of peace.
As the path under the arbour
Bent to the right

The light was bright, revealing
Like a light at the end of a tunnel
The most unique cottage
With flower baskets under each window
Cascading ivy geraniums, lobelia
And other brightly coloured blossoms.
French doors were in the middle

Open wide to another scene within
Of white tiled floor
White wicker chairs
With tables on the side
Accents of blue
Of tiles, vases, and cushions, too.
Filling the space
So perfect for a book or two
Along with a crystal glass or more
To share a classic moment
With a friend
To enjoy the scene
So pure so sublime
The fragrance of the blossoms
The vines and shrubs too
Entwined with a gentle breeze
And the twitter of the garden birds
So pure and true on note.
My dream has seen the reality.

Can a copy be constructed
To be shared with friends
A tea, a lunch, or just to sit
To chat and share
The greatness and the beauty
Of a garden cottage

In a garden
Filled with love
Tea roses and climbers too
A whiff of lemon
Mint and basil three
An herb garden must be near
Glass in hand
A twinkle in the eye
Of mysteries beyond the bend
Drawing me ever deeper
To see beyond the crack
Between the deep blue
Of the garden gate.

05/03/20

SILENCE

Have you stopped in the race of life
To listen for the silence that calms the soul?
Or is your mind humming at speeds uncontrolled
Accompanied by false pressures
Of go, go, go; hurry, hurry, hurry?

Take a moment or two and set aside
60 or 300 seconds or more
And hear the silence of the night,
Away from city life, traffic, people—and
Stuff that never rests—making noise.

Take a drive into the countryside
Find a darkened street
Absent of streetlights or artificial light
That fills the environment
With unnatural sounds and false daylight.

Have you observed the stars in their brilliant sparkle?
Or hear their song as they grace the sky
For us to enjoy and light our way?
Have you stopped to hear the wind across the grass
Or through naked arms of the trees?

Have you heard the song of the winter wind
As it bellows across the fields
Or howls around the corners?
The silence of nature surrounds us
Without a thought or awareness.

To miss the voice of silence
To enrich the mind and thoughts
As the business of life
Traps us in believing what is valuable and true.
In efforts to keep us blind and ignorant of what is real and pure.

Freedom to hear, freedom to see,
Freedom to experience,
Freedom to put down the traps
That occupy our time
To be replaced and hear the beauty of silence.

Have you heard the snow fall
So gently stacking one upon the other?
Have you heard the splash of a raindrop
As it lands from heaven's heights
To grace the land round about?

Have you stopped to hear the gurgling
Of a stream as it tumbles
Over rocks, logs, or nothing
As it races to the ocean
To begin its journey once again?

Have you ever stopped to hear
The growth crackle snap
Of bamboo
Or the summer spurts of corn
During the August heat?

Have you taken a moment to stop and gaze
At trumpeter swans overhead
Gracing the heavens in flight
In a chorus of trumps
Or the slur of gliding feathers one against the other?

Have you heard the chorus of the amphibians,
The frog in a distant water hole?
Or the annoying leg-rubbing cricket
In the trees about?
All of nature's songs a symphony.

Have you heard the tweet
Of a distinct hollow-boned fowl,
The flutter of leaves
From an unseen gentle breeze
Or a rushing wind?

Come, join me in the silence
To hear a world
That most cannot hear
Be filled with a joy
Of unrecognized refreshment.

The silence is never silent
When we place our living
In the light of nature
As its voice calls in rhythms
To grace and bless our noisy busy lives.

01/12/20

EQUINOX

The bright morning sun
Caressing the valley
After bouts of cold and snow
With a tease between rays of sun and bands of warmth

Ah, the crocus in its brilliant colours
Splashing here and there
In shocking deep purple, mauve, yellow, orange, and white
Tickling the anticipation of spring warmth.

Leaves of tulips and daffodils
Standing firm through frosty nights
Filled with an antifreeze
Waiting for the sun to burst their hidden rainbows.

Warmer nights
Windows ajar
Sunshades
Hopes of tan lines to come.

Spring 2019

KISS ME

Kiss me.
Kiss me once kiss me twice.
Kiss me with your soft touch.
Kiss me again on a moonlit night.
Soft and gentle, smooth and supple.

My skin all about tingles
Your arms embrace
Strong and bold
I feel the chill
The shiver and shake of my skin

The embrace so tight
The kiss so cool and fierce
I brace my body
For the next onslaught
A sudden calm or not?

Need I wrap my arms around
To keep the warmth
Or throw a scarf round about?
How refreshed I feel
By the kiss of the winter wind.

01/2019

WIND

What causes the wind to blow
To roar
And then subside
Until another gust evokes its power?

Who tells the wind to cross the land
Over mountains and hills, through valleys, and across the fields?
How does the wind know its speed
And the force that it needs for its time and place?

When does the wind know
To be gentle, with calm
Caressing strokes across the face of the land
With its soft reassuring touch?

Where does the wind know
To go
To move, to shake, to pull
To drag from place to place?

From east or west
North or south
A true mystery to behold
Of the mighty wind that blows.

02/15/20

BECKONING

Have you seen the slant of sunrays—beckoning?
   Have you noticed the snowdrops
   Peeking through the snow
   Nodding their white heads to and fro
   Or the glint of light on wings in flight?

Have you seen the signs of life of hidden bulbs—beckoning?
   As they stretch their arms
   Up high to reach the sky
   A hint, a promise of colour all around
   A joy from splashes of yellow, red, and orange.

Have you seen the breeze at work—beckoning?
   Wrapping warmth all about
   Or feel the tingle of the sun
   As it filters through the barren branches
   Massaging warmth one moment, one day at a time.

Have you seen the swelling buds—beckoning?
   Plump, round, elongated, cracking
   Here, there, and everywhere—a leaf, a flower to be
   Who can tell, as juices flow deep below
   To spring forth seeds for life renewed.

Have you seen the first hue of spring—beckoning?
   All yellow green as buds burst forth
   A hidden golden gem too often unobserved
   A forest glade whose yellow tint
   Soon passes without a thought.

Have you seen the robin pulling on a string—beckoning?
   Stuck halfway in the mud
   A string, some straw, a cotton ball to pad
   To build a home high above
   The bustling, to and fro of human life below.

Have you seen the creator's hand at work today—beckoning?
   Beckoning you and me
   Encouraging us to come
   To come and rest
   And fill our soul with peace.

8/3/18

FALL

Fall is a time of letting go.

However deep the roots go
To let go for a season
To rest

When leaves transition from their vibrant shades of green
Into the rainbow of yellows, oranges, reds, and browns
In time, to release their bonds to their source of sustenance
Sprinkling the earth with colour
And a fragrance that only the autumn season can give

The leaves are but the outer skin
What gives the beauty
Is the core, the root,
The source
That is the supplier of life
Of colour, of character
That brings beauty in every season

Fall is a time to let go
To enjoy the time of rest
To again be energized and come into
The fullness of life with renewed energy
Purpose and drive
To demonstrate boldness and direction
For another season that brings us to Fall

A time to make closure and to rest

11/10/19

TIME TO CELEBRATE

The time is near for celebration
The air is crisp, the mornings cool
Leaves are falling carpeting the ground
Crunching under each step.

The time is near for celebration
When pumpkins and eye-catching gourds
Decorate and stand guard by doors,
Mailboxes, and along sidewalks, too.

The time is near for celebration
When goblins, ghosts, and ghastly things
Appearing to haunt, lurk, and scare
The soul to death yet living

A night that echoes sounds
That freak out those that hear
When spirits come out of hiding
Delighting in the screams of the unsuspecting.

A night so devilish
That releases tricks not treats
Deceiving innocent behaviour
As just a night of fun.

Contrary to the thought
Just a drop of candy in a bag
A subtle promotion for the night
That worships Satan to all extremes.

A time of celebration with sacrificed lives
The drinking of human blood
The eating of human flesh
Done below the surface in secret worldwide.

Though fear and dread fills the air
There is an unearthly awakening
Of the movement of another Spirit that
Fills the heart with love not fear or dread.

A Spirit that moves on holy ground
Instilling fear in all that is evil
Demanding respectful worship
Commanding every knee to bow.

When submission is given to this Holy Spirit
Joy, peace, and love fill the void
That would otherwise be filled
With dread, fear, anxiety, and more

Shadows carry no frightful image
All spells are void of power
Superstitions flee and are gone
Releasing the soul of bondage

No fear of tombs, skulls, or skeletons
No vampire, warlock, werewolf, witch, or wizard
To haunt the hidden corners
Of our earthly life

The time to celebrate is now
Not of evil but that which is good
Pure and holy, to be filled
To emanate the consequence of the blood of the Lamb

10/28/19

*

***

Christmas

Christmas, Christmas, Christmas
What to do?
Where to go?
What to give?

Christmas, Christmas, Christmas
Decorations yes or no?
Should lights be hung?
Or place glass balls in a jar?

Christmas, Christmas, Christmas
Do I travel or stay at home?
Should I write or send a card?
Will the postal service be open to send on time?

Christmas, Christmas, Christmas
Why fret?
Relax.
Enjoy the quiet
Fill the heart
And your soul
With peace

Allow the moment of the season to share Christ Jesus's love to draw
others into the fold

12/2018

FOR OTHERS OR FOR ME?

And so the season of celebration approaches again with a sigh.
Dinners to plan. Invites to be sent.
Invites received to parties and gatherings,
Plays and performances to attend.
Some formal some quite casual,
All with a flair of celebration, excitement, and splash.
Gifts to buy. What to buy?
Menus to plan. Groceries to buy.
Decorations to hang. Wreaths to refurbish.
Garlands to drape over mantels and doors.
Lights to twinkle here and there and along roof lines, too.
Oh, and of course a tree with all its trimmings,
Of lights and streamers, balls and treasures of the past,
To hang here, there, and tucked in behind.
Followed by something special to symbolize
The time when a star stood guard in the sky
Over a child that was born some 2000 years before.
Apple cider is brewing
For carolers who come to sing a tune or two.
Am I set for this busy time of year?

Time is spent for others to be pleased,
But what about me?
Did I put aside time to relax and reflect
On the Saviour who came just for me?
Who grew and lived life as a man but was God.
To be teased and tortured again and again
To be mocked and humiliated and to be hung in shame
For me.
For me to be set free from the enslavement of sin.
To be free to live life without any shame.
May the light so shine
That others may see the Light of the World
Through all the efforts or none
That is done this season to celebrate
What is worthy most of all,
The Christ child that came to set us all free.

27/11/2019

HOWLING WHITE

The days are short
The nights are long

The days are cold
The nights are colder

All the while
The gusting winds

Grip the land
With fierce control

Frozen white crystals
Whip across the land

Horizontal uncontrolled
Drifts accumulating

In open spaces
Eyes open wide

Ploughing through clouds
On four rubber wheels

Hesitation and a shift
To the left or right

But onward go
A destination to reach

Wow, chunks of ice
With wind power

Slid across iced roads
The Spark slid, too

The land gripped
In frozen white

Unrelenting
Days on end

It will pass
The sun will shine

The snow will melt
Rivulets abound

The soil as a sponge
The aquifer below fills

Droplets fall
Heaven to earth

Feeding every tree
Shrub grass and bulb

Bringing beauty
Without measure

Filling the soul
With content

Warmth of sun
Ignites the will

As new life springs forth
A white world renewed

The bone-chilling days
Forgotten once again

No howling winds
No drifts to manoeuver

No bundling up
Restricting movements

But freedom to move
Raising arms in praise

Always thankful
A heart full of gratitude

01/15/20

BE READY

The air is crisp
Nipping at my toes
Colder than the rest
All is good
For my heart is warm
My pulse is strong
In matters of eternity

Rolling down the freeway lanes
An open road
Congestion?
Leaving more focus
To pray
For those the Holy Spirit
Sends my way

To the left and to the right
Words of praise out of delight
As mountains clear and sharp
Stand topped with white
A little more than icing sugar
While down below flitting by
Fields lie in strips of green and white

Wonder above wonder
A glorious day to share
The awesomeness of the living One
Who sits upon the throne
As angels errands run
For saints
And those yet to come in

The road is clear
Patience enthralled
Expectations to behold
As one by one
The barriers fall
Eager for words
Of help and encouragement

A time to drink in wisdom
A time of silence
A time of words for laughter
A time when stress is broken
A time for questions
A time to listen
A time to make most clear

A steady focus
All things clear
Resting assured
Through prayer and petition
And with rejoicing
Spiritual requests presented to the throne
Believe, and it will be yours

06/15/2018

A VISITOR CAME TODAY

A visitor came today
All dressed in metallic attire
Glimmering
To hum
To share life's beauty and grace
As I sat in silence
On the terrace
Flitting from one to the other
With speeds blurred to the naked eye
Floating in space
Still, as if frozen
Then to dart
Was gone
Leaving me enthralled with anticipation
Of further visits to interrupt my day.

06/24/2020

GARDEN TWO

Step by step
Round and round
Descending
One step at a time
A Venetian garden
Surrounds
Upright, draping, cascading
Twisting, clinging
Strawberries
A bench to sit
Blue cushions for comfort
Tomatoes
All around perennials
Colours abound
Blueberries
A square stone to welcome
A mailbox standing proud
Plants
All about to make it home
Across the way there is more
Roses
Red, yellow, pink
Double and triple colours abound
Foxglove
In between columbine
With singular and double colours
Contrasting
Black, purple and white, royal purple
Too many more to name
Home
Where the Spirit dwells
To be filled with a calm
Peace
Across the lane a step or two

An edible garden full
Infancy
Time for growth
Harvest multiplied
Abundance
Squash, gourds, and more
Peas, beets, carrots, scallions
Leeks
Pole beans, cabbage—red and green
Row upon row of onions
Lettuce galore
Bush beans and corn
Not to forget the cauliflower and broccoli
Plenty
A plate to fill
A stomach to satisfy
Gardens
To satiate the soul
Tranquility saturate
Calm
All for a season
A whisper to hold

06/06/2020

I SAW A WOLF

At the quietest time of the night
It was dark
In the middle of the barnyard
The yard light on
As always
A swallow or two of water
A blind stare through the kitchen window
Drinking glass in hand
Right hip against the counter

Not a leaf from the maple
Standing tall
Just outside the walls of the tree house
It was winter
No shadows

There, standing tall
Dark
Black
Against the gravel
Flooded with bright light
Head erect like a llama
But dog in stature
Furry
Long-haired

Shaking my head
Is it real?
A second look
Both hands on the counter
Staring

Not a muscle moved
By both
He, it, frozen
Sighting in the distance
Something of interest
Placing the glass down
Eyes diverted
For a second
The wolf was gone.

06/12/2020

Academic

A dear colleague wrote these words in response to the sharing of
my poetry as an encouragement to the many international
students that came to my office for academic and personal support.
I am very grateful and thankful of her generous spirit, kind heart
and commitment to living life serving the living God.

The following poem is an awesome door to open the poems
dedicated to my academic world.

A usual friendly open door
And very welcoming to the core,
A mentor with a sense of humour
and a vigorous demeanour
He welcomes you into his green cave,
Yes, apprentice, please be brave!
To share concerns, life stories, academic struggles,
He will try to find a righteous way
To keep away your troubles!

Olya (Volha) Kliuyeva

SPACES

The door, usually open
An invitation to stop by
To sit, to study, to chat
To share life's closets
When the door is shut

To hear a word of insight, guidance

The door, when closed
No interruptions please
An indication for private time
For marking, for research, for planning
A dynamic presentation

The power of words, graphs, charts, media—ah—the understanding

The door, what door?
An open space bare and exposed
Voices carry, louder than intent
To guide, to lead, to direct
A space of living greens

How to be when so exposed

The door, mostly open
Fresh air in high demand
Did you read the sign?
Fragrance Free if you please
Or death may take its hold

A frightful thought to not instruct or interact

The door, closed or ajar
My presence known but just a whisper
In my little space
Quietly to instruct and guide
Leadership in waiting

To lead the world what a fright

The door often closed or just a crack
To protect my space
From pollutants that disgrace
But mainly prepping lessons
Giving feedback with no end

A Godly joy as understanding grows

Each space unique, coveted by a door or not
Each in high demand
To express, this is me, this is mine
Living plants, family portraits
Art decor of travels, or places once called home

Spaces unique to me and to you

2018

A CHILD BORN TODAY

A young lady bold and strong in character
Entered with a sigh
"Oh, I am not well. I am sick today."
She was down and sad.

"Well, we need to do something about that."
No sympathy from me
"Oh, I have been working on a paper …
I used lots of quotes from the Bible.
That book is so good."

Scrolling down the touch screen
Examples of biblical citations
Oops, there are two sentences beginning with "So" …

"When writing this paper
I really wanted to become a Christian
But I don't know how."

"Well, that is easy."
"Really?"
"Yes, of course. Let me show you."

On the table a paper came
Of an A B C
Of becoming a believer
Admit to the sinner that I am
Believe and accept Jesus is God
Who died for your sins.
Call to God in prayer.
Confess your sins
Saved you now are
When truly done from the heart.

"That is it?"
"That is all."
"Oh, I want to be a follower of God.
I want to be a Christian …

… A prayer …
How exciting. I have found my way.
I found my belief."

And so the hour went
When the time to leave drew nigh
The symptoms of the cold were gone
As all thoughts on God were foremost
And a joy filled the void
That was present for years.
A longing filled
Through the power of the Holy Spirit
Creating a princess in training
To meet her Father the King
Through life's adventures and
Journeys
Right to the end.

10/23/2019

SUMMER CAMP

Rolling down the freeway in a yellow school bus
Lifting up a thought of prayer for every face and name to match
Wondering through all this business
What would be remembered when this summer trip is complete.

Will it be the smell of the sweets
The raw farm smells or
Sticky's?
Will it be the cobbled stones of Gastown or
The swinging bridge in Capilano?
The adventure to Hell's Gate and the fudge or
The summer rain in Hope and the pavilion?
Will it be the games or
The tying of knots or
The playing of soccer in the summer sun?
Would it be the placing of puzzle pieces together with many hands or
The putting at Tapin's or
The morning language lessons?
Will it be the conversations or
The farewell party?
The food or the homestay families?
Will this summer be remembered
In five or ten years?
Two weeks were filled.

                    07/15/2015

OVERSEAS CANADIAN SUMMER CAMP

I heard about a God
That they say is alive.
Do I need to know him?
Can I live without this God
That seems to be so real
In every homestay member?
Three weeks have passed so quickly.
What will I take home
From this cool summer camp
Of 2016?

08/2016

WORDS, WORDS, AND MORE WORDS

Oh, my God! Help me!
The demands for words are all around
Words to utter
Words to compose
Words in a tongue foreign to my roots
Words to gather in coherent order
Words with deadlines
Words, words, and more words

They are coming out of my ears.

Can they be composed into comprehensible form?
Can the native speaker decipher my intent?
Can I express my thoughts with clarity?
Can I reach the mark
    The mark to see me through?

Ah! Remember the words!
    "Ask and you shall receive."
    "Pray as if you have already received,
        and it shall be yours."*

Yes! Oh yes. Faith. The key. Total faith. Total surrender.

        Thank you!

And the words came
In precision

The joy of another lesson learned.

                    03/09/2018

* Mark 11:24

HERE TODAY, GONE TOMORROW

One day, I, too, will be gone to be with our heavenly Father.
No tears are needed, but for some it will be sad. If we continue in
the footsteps that Jesus made, sharing his love and inviting others to
join in the line of saints that have asked for forgiveness of their sins,
and walk in the Holy Spirit's love and compassion, there is nothing lost,
but everything is gained. What a glorious day that will be when the
reunions, not of classmates (though some may be there, too) but of the
Saints that have surrendered all to give God the glory as best they can
with what they had, and we celebrate God's greatness round about the
throne and elsewhere in the heavenly heights yonder. What a day to
look forward to when our spot is ready and our call to come home is
given. Be blessed and encouraged as we still travel these roads of life,
sharing and witnessing so that his glory shines, till all that are
written in the Book of Life are called.

Printed in Canada